All rights reserved
978-1-7394545-4-8
First impression, 2023
Wooden House Books
www.woodenhousebooks.com

Understanding anxiety and managing feelings

The Kids' Book of
WORRIES

Catherine and Jenny Stephenson.
Illustrated by Hiruni Kariyawasam

We all have lots
of different feelings.

Sometimes we feel happy, other times we might feel sad, angry, excited, confused... and all sorts of other feelings! Our feelings change a lot - it's part of being human.

Can you think of any words to describe the feelings shown on the opposite page?

We can learn to listen to our feelings, and guess what? They can actually help us in lots of ways.

One feeling is worry.

Worry is when you are thinking a lot about something that makes you feel unsure or scared.

Worries can make you feel sad or uncomfortable. They might make you feel like you want to hide or run away.

It's normal to have worries. Everyone worries sometimes, grown-ups too!

Worry is actually a special way your body tries to keep you safe.

Other names for worry are anxiety (feeling anxious) or scared.

Our bodies feel worries in different ways.

Sometimes, you might not know if you're feeling worried. But, if you pay attention to your body, it can give you clues.

You might notice your heart beating faster or have a funny tummy, feel shaky, your muscles might feel tight, you could start to sweat, or even find it tricky to fall asleep.

Where do you feel worries in your body?

Activity: Find a pencil and a piece of paper! Start by drawing a picture of yourself. Then, draw where you feel worries.

Different things can make people feel worried.

making friends

big dogs or
other animals

when things change

monsters

saying goodbye
to a parent

loud noises

starting something
new

being away from
family

the dark

Can you remember a time when
you felt worried about something?

It's okay to notice when you feel worried.

Sometimes worries disappear all by
themselves, other times they take
a little longer to go away.

The great news is there are things you
can do to help yourself feel better, and a
grown-up can help you practice these.

Let's look through these ideas next.

HELP FOR YOUR
WORRIES

Share your worries.

When we talk to someone we trust,
like a grown-up or a friend, just talking
about our worries out loud can make
them feel smaller and less scary.

They might give us comforting words
or helpful ideas, and we won't feel alone.

Some children might need extra help
from an adult who is trained to help
children with worries, and that's okay too.

Healthy habits.

Looking after your body can help you feel better when you're worried.

EAT

If you eat healthy foods, they can give you energy and help you feel good. They can also help your brain work better and help you feel more able to manage things.

MOVE

Doing exercise, like running, jumping, or playing games, helps our bodies feel strong and happy. It can make us feel more relaxed and calm.

SLEEP

Sleep helps to recharge our brains. After a good night's sleep, we are more able to manage our worries.

Just breathe!

Taking slow and deeper breaths
can help you feel calmer.

1. Find a quiet and comfortable place to sit or lie down. Close your eyes if it helps you focus.

2. Imagine you are smelling a lovely flower, and take a slow breath in through your nose, filling up your tummy like a balloon.

3. Then, slowly breathe out through your mouth, like you're blowing out candles on a birthday cake.

4. Repeat this, taking nice, slow breaths in and out.

Can you practice this with an adult? How does it make you both feel?

Your 5 senses.

When you're feeling worried, it can help to pay attention to what's around you.

Find somewhere to sit, relax your body and breathe.

Now find...

5 things you can see

4 things you can feel
(like the ground beneath your
feet, your clothes, a breeze)

3 things you can hear

2 things you can smell

1 thing you can taste

3 good things.

Did you know that even on days when we feel more worried, there are still good things that happen?

Before you go to bed, think of 3 good things that happened today. It can be the tiniest thing, like something nice your teacher said, a fun game or splashing in a puddle. Maybe everybody in your family could could take turns to share their 3 good things?

Imagine your happy place.

Think of a place where you have felt safe, comfortable or relaxed.

Find somewhere quiet, and close your eyes for a minute or two. Now imagine your happy place. What do you see? What do you hear? What do you smell?

You could also try doing this when you're feeling worried.

Notice what helps
you relax.

What do you love doing?
It could be an activity that
makes you feel calm or happy.
It might be drawing, playing a
sport, reading a book, dancing,
or playing with toys.

Get creative.

Writing down your feelings or drawing a picture can help make you feel better and less worried.

If you want to, you can show your picture or writing to someone you trust.

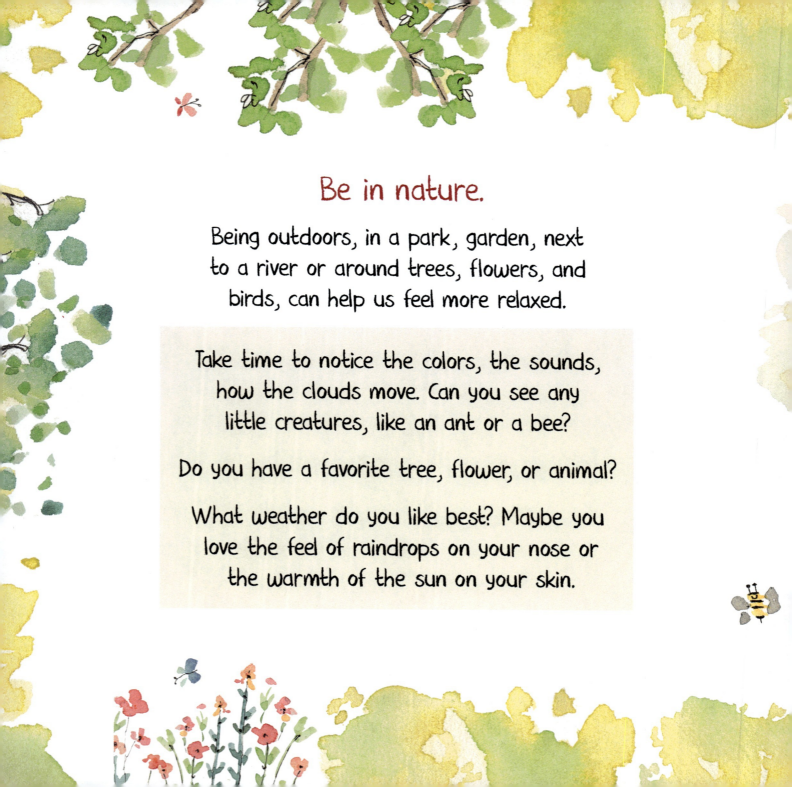

Be in nature.

Being outdoors, in a park, garden, next to a river or around trees, flowers, and birds, can help us feel more relaxed.

Take time to notice the colors, the sounds, how the clouds move. Can you see any little creatures, like an ant or a bee?

Do you have a favorite tree, flower, or animal?

What weather do you like best? Maybe you love the feel of raindrops on your nose or the warmth of the sun on your skin.

My worry jar.

A worry jar is a place for children to put their worries so they don't have to think about them all the time.

Find an empty, clean jar, and decorate it. Make it bright and colorful, with stickers, ribbons or paint!

WORRY JAR

Whenever you feel worried about something, write it on a piece of paper. Put it in your worry jar, and try and let go of your worry.

I'm worried about a new teacher.

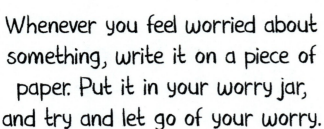
scary monsters

I've fallen out with my friend.

I felt silly in front of the class

Keep your jar somewhere you can see it. Now, if you feel worried, you can give those worries to the jar to hold onto for you, and you can feel a little bit better.

Practicing brave behavior.

Sometimes facing your fears can help.
Imagine you are scared of spiders. Or
of the dark. Practicing being brave
can help to overcome worries.

To face your fear, start taking
small steps. For example,
you could play hide and seek
in the dark with your family.

Or make shadow puppets!

Is there anything new you'd like to do? Maybe you can practice taking small steps towards this. What might this practicing look like?

Will my worries go away?

With practice, it gets easier to manage
our worries. Finding how to deal with
worries is something we learn
about all through our lives.

Grown-ups are learning too! Maybe you
could ask your grown-up about a time
they felt worried and what helped them?

Which did you like the most?

Put a tick or draw a smiley face next to the activities you liked most.

- [ ] Share your worries
- [ ] Healthy habits
- [ ] Just breathe!
- [ ] Your 5 senses
- [ ] 3 good things
- [ ] Your happy place
- [ ] Notice what helps you relax
- [ ] Get creative
- [ ] Be in nature
- [ ] My worry jar
- [ ] Practicing brave behavior

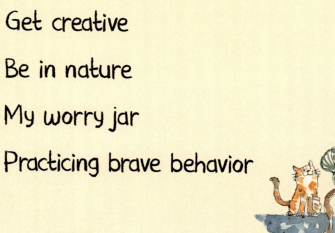

Dear Reader,

Thank you for choosing to read *The Kids' Book of Worries* with your child – I hope you found it helpful. If you could spare a few minutes to leave me a review on Amazon, I'd love to recieve your feedback.

This book forms part of The Kids' Books of Social Emotional Learning series, which also includes:

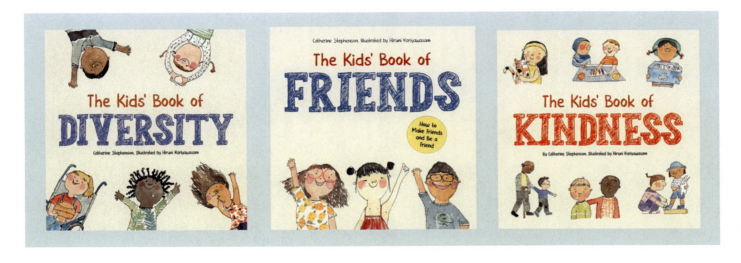

Thank you so much for your support and interest in our books!

Catherine
woodenhousebooks.com

About the authors and the illustrator.

Jenny

Jenny is a chartered educational psychologist based in the UK, with a particular interest in the understanding and management of childhood anxiety. She is experienced in a range of evidenced-based approaches, including cognitive behavioural therapy (CBT), mindfulness and acceptance and commitment therapy. Jenny works with the consultancy Brighter Futures, which provides schools and parents with specialist services to improve learning and well-being outcomes for children. She is also the director of HappySleepers, a psychological service supporting children with anxiety-related sleep difficulties.

Catherine

Catherine is Jenny's sister. They both grew up in Wales, UK. She now lives with her partner, son and two cats in Barcelona, Spain. She is a translator from Spanish and Catalan into English and a children's book author. Her other books include *The Kids' Book of Friends*, *The Kids' Book of Diversity* and *The Kids' Book of Kindness*, all of which she worked on with Hiruni. Away from work, you'll find her in the mountains with a camera round her neck.

Hiruni

Hiruni and Catherine met online in 2022. Hiruni is from Sri Lanka, where she currently lives with her family, in a town called Ambalangoda. She holds a Bachelor's Degree in Fashion Design from the University of Moratuwa. She enjoys doing paintings, fine illustrations, and especially illustrations for children's books in her unique style, mixing digital and watercolour techniques. In her free time, she's also an avid reader.
You can find her on IG: @hiru_k96.

WOODEN HOUSE BOOKS
woodenhousebooks.com
IG @woodenhousebooks

Made in the USA
Las Vegas, NV
30 April 2024

89342418R00024